Published in 2015 by The Rosen Publishing Group, Inc.
29 East 21st Street, New York, NY 10010

Photo Credits: **KEY** tl=top left; tc=top center; tr=top right; cl=center left; c=center; cr=center right; bl=bottom left; bc=bottom center; br=bottom right; bg=background
CBCD = Corbis Photodisc; iS = istockphoto.com; PDCD = PhotoDisc; SH = Shutterstock; TPL = photolibrary.com

6cl iS; **15**tr PDCD; **18**tr iS; **26**tr SH; **30**bg CBCD; c iS; tc, tr, cr, br SH; bc TPL; **31**bg CBCD

All illustrations copyright Weldon Owen Pty Ltd, except **8**c, bc, br; **9**c, br; **10**tl; **20**bc, bl Magic Group

WELDON OWEN PTY LTD
Managing Director: Kay Scarlett
Creative Director: Sue Burk
Publisher: Helen Bateman
Senior Vice President, International Sales: Stuart Laurence
Vice President Sales North America: Ellen Towell
Administration Manager, International Sales: Kristine Ravn

Library of Congress Cataloging-in-Publication Data

McFadzean, Lesley., author.
 Birds : flying high / by Lesley McFadzean.
     pages cm. — (Discovery education. Animals)
 Includes index.
 ISBN 978-1-4777-6930-0 (library binding) — ISBN 978-1-4777-6932-4 (pbk.) — ISBN 978-1-4777-6931-7 (6-pack)
 1. Birds—Juvenile literature. I. Title.
 QL676.2.M387 2015
 598—dc23
                                        2013047452

Manufactured in the United States of America

CPSIA Compliance Information: Batch #WS14PK3: For Further Information contact Rosen Publishing, New York, New York at 1-800-237-9932

BIRDS
FLYING HIGH

Lesley McFadzean

PowerKiDS press

New York

Contents

Bird Evolution

Birds evolved from reptiles, probably from a group of small, meat-eating dinosaurs known as theropods. These dinosaurs shared some of the same features as birds. They laid eggs, and their internal organs and some of their bones were similar to those of birds. Reptiles have scales made of a substance called keratin and birds have feathers made of the same material. A sparrow may not look anything like a dinosaur but an ostrich does.

That's Amazing!

Scientist Thomas Huxley noticed a small extra bone on a quail's leg that he was eating. It was the same as one he had seen on a dinosaur fossil, and he realized they were related.

Fossil feathers
Archaeopteryx was the first fossilized animal with feathers and wings that was ever found.

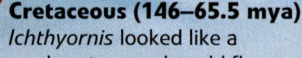

Cretaceous (146–65.5 mya)
Ichthyornis looked like a modern tern and could fly better than *Archaeopteryx*.

Jurassic (200–146 mya)
Archaeopteryx looked like a dinosaur, but it had feathered wings and could fly.

Triassic (251–200 mya)
Small theropods were fast runners, but they had no feathers and no wings.

Links in the chain

Theropod dinosaurs had strong back legs and small front limbs used to catch prey. Millions of years ago (mya), these front limbs adapted to become wings.

Modern period
Over millions of years, birds have developed the features needed for faster and longer flights.

SKELETONS OVER TIME

Some theropod dinosaurs had a collarbone and breastbone fused together, like birds do. Their hips pointed downward, like birds' hips. Their short front limbs had flexible wrists. As birds evolved, these wrists were used for the downstroke of wings.

Dinosaur
Some scientists think that *Compsognathus* is a possible ancestor of birds.

Archaeopteryx
Archaeopteryx had the back legs and toothed jaw of a dinosaur, but it had wings.

Modern bird
Unlike its ancestors, it has a short, bony tail, shorter legs, and larger breastbone.

Land Birds

There are more than 9,000 species of birds. All have feathers, a beak, and no teeth, and they all lay eggs with hard shells. But birds live in many different habitats. Some bird species, like the birds shown here, live only on land. They are terrestrial birds.

Gray-striped francolin
The francolin is a large, stout, forest bird. It is related to the partridge and the quail.

Wedge-billed hummingbird
This tiny bird lives in cloud forests high in the Andes, in South America.

Northern hawk owl
Small rodents and birds are the main food of this forest-dwelling owl.

Quetzal
The quetzal's brilliant tail feathers can grow to 2 feet (60 cm).

Spotted puffbird
Perched on a low branch, the spotted puffbird sits still and waits for prey.

Black-rumped woodpecker
This woodpecker forages for insects in the woodlands of India.

Vulture
The vulture is a scavenger that feeds mainly on the bodies of dead animals.

Eclectus parrot
The female eclectus parrot is bright red and the male is bright green.

Emerald dove
This dove eats fruits and seeds on the forest floor of rain forests in Asia, New Guinea, and Australia.

Hook-billed kingfisher
The rain forests of New Guinea are home to this whistling kingfisher.

UNUSUAL EMU
Australian emus can grow up to 6 feet (1.8 m) tall. Shaggy feathers droop down on both sides of their body.

Shaggy feathers hang down.

Cock-of-the-rock
When this bird of the rain forest flies, its flight feathers make a hissing noise.

Saffron finch
This small yellow finch grows to 6 inches (15 cm) long.

Each foot has three toes.

Waterbirds

There are two types of waterbirds. Freshwater birds live in swamps and marshes—often called wetlands—or near lakes, ponds, or rivers. Seabirds live in and around the oceans. But waterbirds do not spend all of their lives in water because most nest on land. For freshwater birds, reed beds, holes in riverbanks, or trees near water make good nesting sites. For seabirds, cliffs, ocean islands, and mangroves are possible nesting sites.

Dalmatian pelican
The pelican's large wings allow it to glide as well as fly. Gliding conserves energy as it takes less effort than flying.

Food for all
Some seabirds dig shellfish from the sand. Some grab fish from the surface of the water, while others dive deep.

Little egrets
Long legs keep their feathers out of water.

Cory's shearwater

Great tern

Little tern

Greater flamingo
The flamingo has long legs for wading. It drags its neck through the water and filters shellfish into its open mouth.

Goliath heron
This large African heron stalks prey. It wades quietly through the water, then stabs a fish with its dagger-like beak.

Black-necked stork
This stork's wingspan is more than 7 feet (2.1 m).

Brolga
The dancing brolga feeds on plants and insects.

Inside Birds

A bird's internal anatomy has some special features that allow the bird to fly. It has fewer—and lighter—bones than a mammal so that it can get off the ground. It also has a special digestive system. Birds are the only animals that have a crop for storing some of their food instead of digesting it right away. This allows a bird to store the energy it needs for flight without overloading its stomach or gizzard. Bird lungs, which breathe in and out in time with the bird's wing beats, are connected to special air sacs. These air sacs also make the bird's body lighter.

Did You Know?

Birds eat more food in proportion to the size of their bodies than most animals. Some birds eat as much as 80 percent of their body weight in a single day.

Esophagus

Crop

Liver

Intestines

Gizzard

Cloaca

Feeding
Birds have a crop that stores food, then passes small amounts down to the gizzard where it is ground up.

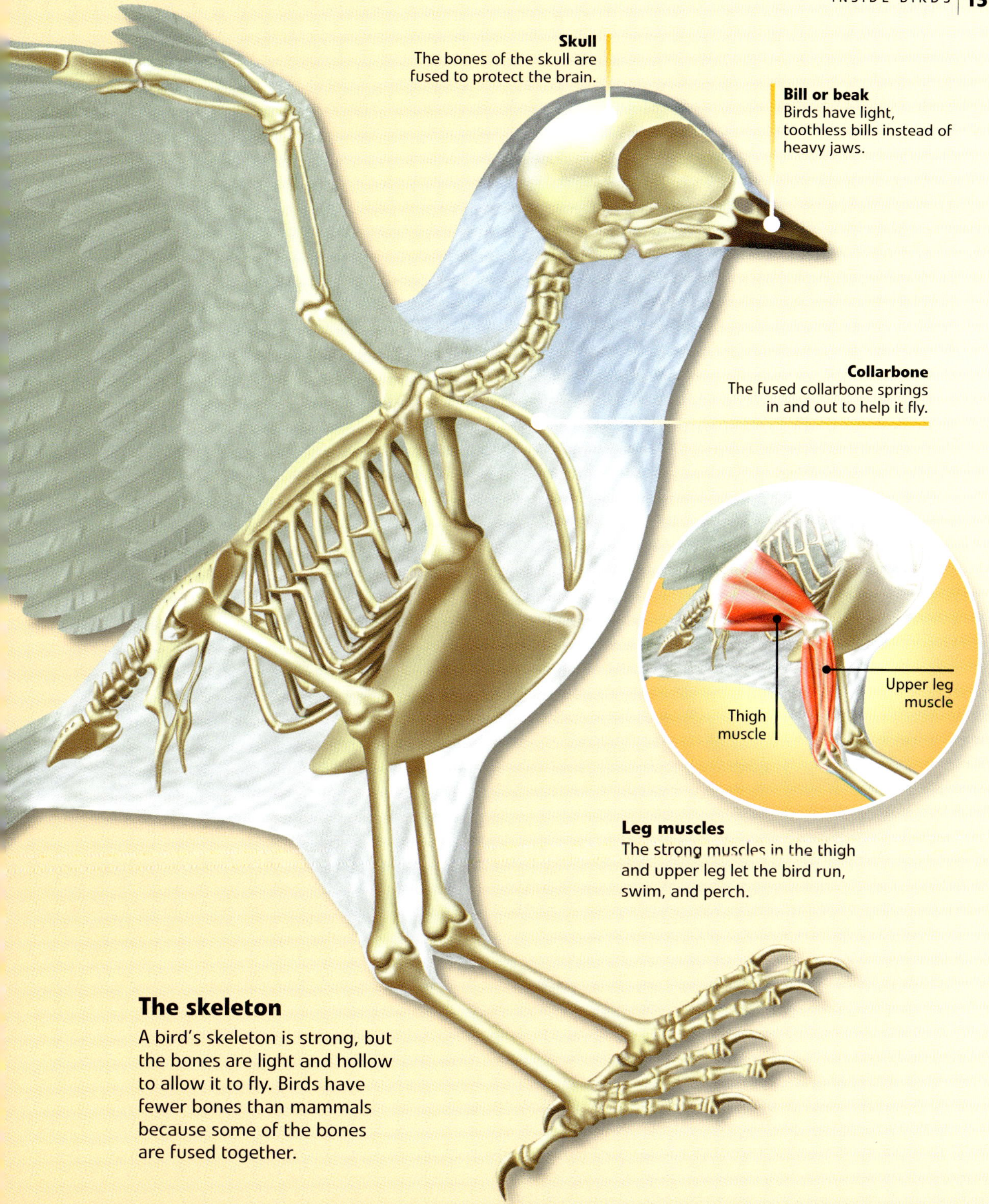

Skull
The bones of the skull are fused to protect the brain.

Bill or beak
Birds have light, toothless bills instead of heavy jaws.

Collarbone
The fused collarbone springs in and out to help it fly.

Upper leg muscle

Thigh muscle

Leg muscles
The strong muscles in the thigh and upper leg let the bird run, swim, and perch.

The skeleton

A bird's skeleton is strong, but the bones are light and hollow to allow it to fly. Birds have fewer bones than mammals because some of the bones are fused together.

Feathers

Birds are the only animals with feathers, and these come in every color of the rainbow. Colored feathers are used as camouflage and to attract mates. Birds' feathers overlap and point backward, from head to tail, so that the wind passes smoothly over them during flight. When a feather becomes worn or damaged, a new feather beneath it pushes out the old feather. This process is known as molting. Most birds replace their feathers twice a year but not all at the same time!

TYPES OF FEATHERS

Soft, downy feathers next to the skin keep the bird warm. On top of these are short, round contour feathers that give the bird its streamlined shape and color. Long flight feathers are in the wings and tail. The shaft down the center of a feather has barbs that hold the feather together smoothly.

Shaft with barbs

Long tail feather

Contour feather

Downy feather

Tail feathers

Did You Know?

The ruby-throated hummingbird has only 940 feathers, which is fewer than any other bird. The whistling swan has the most feathers—up to 25,000 feathers in winter.

Blue bird–of–paradise
The males work very hard to attract a mate. They hang upside down, fluff up their breast feathers, and let their black tail plumes hang down.

The peacock's "eyes"
This bird's long tail feathers, called coverts, can be up to 60 percent of its body length. The colorful "eye" markings are for attracting females.

Crest feathers

Crown feathers

Overlapping feathers
The blue jay's feathers neatly overlap each other. No feathers are out of place. If they were, they would catch in the wind and slow the bird's flight.

Victoria crowned pigeon
The world's largest pigeon has beautiful, lacy crest feathers. These feathers are used to attract a mate. Unfortunately, they also attract hunters.

Greater coverts

Lesser coverts

Flight feathers

Wings

Wing shapes vary to suit the environment the bird lives in and the kind of flying it does. Short, round wings are good in tight spaces such as forests because they do not catch on trees or plants. But they are not good for speed or long flights. Short, pointed wings, such as a swift's wings, are ideal for flying in open sky at high speeds. Long, thin wings are built for slow, long-distance flying and also for hovering, soaring, and gliding. Many seabirds, including the albatross, have these wings. Slots, which are called fingers, at the end of the wings help birds to maneuver at slow speeds.

WINGSPANS

A bird's wingspan is measured from the tip of one wing right across to the tip of the other wing when both of the wings are fully open.

Stork
Wingspan: 60 inches (150 cm)

Duck
Wingspan: 20 inches (55 cm)

Swift
Wingspan: 13 inches (33 cm)

Sparrow
Wingspan: 9 inches (22 cm)

Silent wings
Nocturnal owls are silent fliers. The edges of their wings have gaps or fringes that let air pass through their feathers silently. This helps them hunt.

Huge wingspan
The open wings of six swallows fit across one half of the 11-foot (3.4-m) wingspan of the wandering albatross. The albatross can "lock" its opened wings into position.

Albatross body weight
The wings carry a body that weighs 18 pounds (8 kg).

Eastern rosella
This rosella is red, green, and yellow ... until it flies. Only then do its blue flight feathers become visible.

Hunter's wings
A black heron can throw its wings over its head like a cloak. The shadow this casts helps the heron to see into the water and the shade attracts fish.

Birds in Flight

Flight feathers, wing muscles, and a streamlined shape are all needed for flight. A bird's primary flight feathers, which are also called remiges, are on the outside of the wing. The secondary flight feathers are the wing feathers closer to the body. The strong flight feathers in the tail are called rectrices. The two strong flight muscles are attached to the sternum, or breastbone. One muscle pulls the wing downward, the other muscle raises it. The bird's shape, backward-facing feathers, and legs that tuck up make it streamlined for flight.

Diving
Many birds dive at great speed to catch prey in the water by surprise.

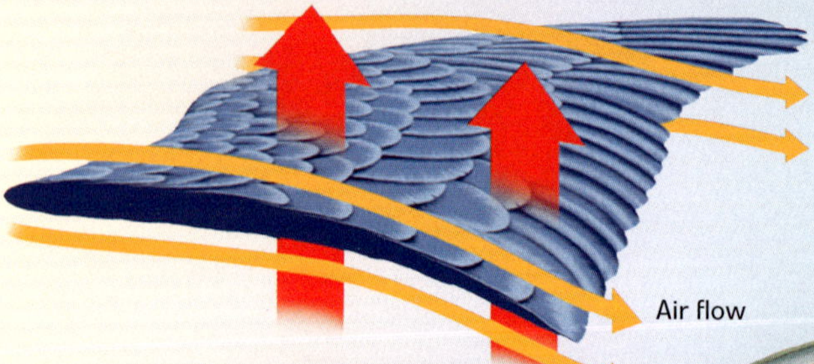

Air flow

Air flow

Uplift

Air flow around a wing
Air flows faster across the curved top surface of the wing and there is less pressure. The difference in pressure with the underside of the wing gives uplift.

Wings at work
A bird does not only flap its wings up and down to fly. It can open or close its flight feathers. It can also hold its wings close in to its body or stretch them away from it.

2 Upstroke
The upstroke continues with the wings above and close to the bird's body.

1 Start
The European robin starts to lift its wings. The flight feathers open to let air pass through.

Flight engine
Two sets of muscles on the breast drive the wings up and down.

THE HUMMINGBIRD

It has the fastest wing beats—100 per second. It can fly forward, back, down, up, sideways, or it can hover.

Downstroke to move forward

Upstroke also to move forward

Figure-of-eight strokes to hover

Backward stroke

4 Downstroke
As the wings push down against the air, these propel the bird forward.

5 End
At the end of the downstroke, the flight feathers open to reduce drag.

3 Stretched out
The wings are stretched out to their full extent. The legs are tucked under the body.

Flightless Birds

Flightless birds are birds that cannot fly. Some of these birds have wings, without flight feathers, but none of them has the muscles needed to move their wings in flight. Without these muscles, flightless birds have a flatter chest than other birds. Some flightless birds may have lost their ability to fly because it was not necessary. Many of them evolved in isolated environments where there were no predators to fly away from. When predators did arrive, flightless birds became extinct. But some survived because of their large size or their ability to outrun or outswim predators.

Penguins underwater
Penguins have flippers instead of wings. They cannot fly or run. But in the water they can swim up to 20 miles (32 km) per hour.

Ostrich
The ostrich cannot fly, but it can outrun an antelope at speeds of up to 40 miles (65 km) per hour.

Cassowary
The cassowary lives in the rain forests of Australia, where the thick undergrowth makes it difficult to use large wings.

That's Amazing!

The ostrich is the world's biggest bird. It has fluffy wings, but they could never lift its enormous body weight of 280 pounds (127 kg) into the air.

New Zealand

The islands of New Zealand were formed 80–100 mya. New Zealand has many flightless birds and most of them are endangered.

Kakapo
This is the world's largest parrot and the only parrot that cannot fly.

Kiwi
The brown kiwi has poor eyesight but a good sense of smell.

Takahe
The takahe nests on the ground. It has powerful legs and feet.

Weka
The weka has wings but they are used only for balance when it runs.

Bird bills are made of keratin. Bird feathers and human fingernails are made of it, too.

TOUCAN

The toco toucan is the largest of all 37 toucan species. It lives in the canopy of South American rain forest trees. Its bill is almost 8 inches (20 cm) long, but it is very light because there are air pockets inside it.

Picking fruits

The toucan uses its bill to pick fruits from high branches. It then throws back its head and swallows the fruits.

Habitat and Diet

Blue tit

The blue tit eats insects in summer and seeds in winter, when there are few insects.

Some birds eat only plants, seeds, and fruits. Others eat insects. Waterbirds eat fish, while birds of prey eat meat. Different species can share the same habitat because they are looking for different foods in different parts of it—on the ground, in treetops, under bark, in mud, sand, or nearby water. Bill shapes are clues to a bird's preferred diet. Strong bills are made for crushing or hammering. Hooked bills are good for tearing. Long, narrow bills are used to dig up or spear food.

Atlantic puffin
This seabird eats up to 40 fish a day. Its stout beak and the spines on the roof of its mouth are ideal for holding slippery fish, which it swallows whole.

Nesting

Birds know, without being taught, what kind of nest to build and how to build it. Some species weave very intricate nests, while others build simple nests of sticks. Some species nest in cavities (holes) in wood, mud, or a cliff face. Others make do with a scrape on the ground. The nesting bird, or birds, must first decide where to build the nest. Then they collect nest materials that include sticks, stones, feathers, hair, and cobwebs. Finally, they build the nest that will keep their eggs warm and safe from predators.

Ground nest
Black-winged stilts nest in colonies. They build mounds of vegetation near freshwater.

Cup nest
Most birds that nest in trees make cup nests so their eggs do not roll out of the tree.

Aerie
Birds of prey make nests called aeries, which they rebuild and add to, year after year.

Hanging basket
The male black-headed weaver builds its nest from grass and other plant material. It weaves, stitches, and knots this together then displays the nest—and itself—to attract female birds.

BURROW NEST
Some waterbirds make a burrow in the mud of a riverbank. They must make sure the nest is above the water level during flooding.

A kingfisher burrow nest

Migration

In winter, almost half of all bird species migrate from cold areas, which are far from the equator, to warm, tropical areas. Most birds migrate in flocks, although a few species migrate alone. They stop off on the way to rest and feed, usually at the same place and at the same time every year. The major migration routes are known as flyways and often follow coastlines, mountain ranges, or river valleys. Scientists think that birds use these landscape features as well as the Sun, Moon, and stars to navigate along the same route every year.

Flamingos
Flamingos fly mainly at night when they migrate. With good tailwinds, they can cover 375 miles (600 km) in one night.

Geese in flight
Geese usually migrate in large flocks that fly in a V formation. Each bird saves energy by flying in the wind currents, or vortex, created by the wings of the bird in front of it.

Rufous
hummingbird

Bobolink

Barn
swallow

Common
cuckoo

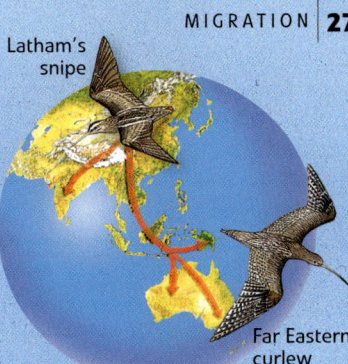

Latham's
snipe

Far Eastern
curlew

The Americas
There are many routes
between North and South
America. These are like
tributaries that merge
into overlapping flyways.

Europe to Africa
Millions of soaring birds,
songbirds, and waterbirds
travel along the flyways
from Europe and Asia to
Africa each year.

Asia to Australia
The flyway from East Asia
to Australia crosses
22 countries. Waterbirds
make a round trip of
16,200 miles (26,000 km).

Did You Know?
Birds prepare for migration. They
eat more to get extra fat reserves
and energy. They make sure their
feathers are in good condition, often
molting just before they leave.

Endangered

Animal predators and diseases can endanger birds. But the main reason that birds become endangered is human activity. When trees are cut down to sell as logs or to clear land for a new town, road, train track, or pipeline, birds lose their habitat and their food supply. Some birds are hunted for their colored feathers, for the pet trade, or for food. Climate change is also a problem. Rising sea levels flood nesting land and freshwater becomes salty. Rising air temperatures dry up the wetlands where birds rest during migration.

Did You Know?

When European explorers arrived in Hawaii in 1778, there were about 25,000 Hawaiian geese. By about the 1950s, only 30 were left. With breeding programs, there are now 3,000 geese.

Gouldian finch
This finch eats only grass seeds in Australian tropical woodlands. Now cattle and horses graze, and the grass no longer seeds.

White-headed duck
This duck breeds among the reeds in wetlands. It is endangered because of habitat loss and duck hunting.

Royal penguin
This penguin is found only on Macquarie Island, off Australia. Pollution, fishing, and climate change now endanger it.

Harpy eagle
The biggest risk to the survival of the harpy eagle of South America is the destruction of its rain forest habitat.

Gone forever
During the past 330 years about 100 bird species have become extinct. The main cause was the arrival of non-native predators.

Dodo
The large, flightless dodo was extinct by 1680. There are a few illustrations and some bones in museums, but no one will ever see a live dodo again.

Passenger pigeon
The last passenger pigeon in the wild disappeared in September 1899. The bird became extinct when the last captive pigeon, in Cincinnati Zoo, died in 1914.

Golden parakeet
Hunters trap these endangered birds while they are roosting. They sell the birds as pets or sometimes they sell their feathers.

Great auk
In 1844, the last great auk was killed in Iceland. Great auks were often hunted for food or for their down. They were also killed by fishermen for bait.

Fact File

Alexander Wetmore was the first ornithologist to classify birds into families, genera, and species. Some species have features that make them stand out from other birds.

1 The Australian pelican has the largest beak of any bird. It grows up to 18.5 inches (47 cm) long and can hold 3 gallons (13 l) of water.

2 Eagles have four sharp talons on each foot. When the eagle catches prey, its strong leg muscles close the talons together like a vise.

3 The African jacana is also known as the "Jesus bird" because it appears to walk on water.

4 The peregrine falcon can fly 60 miles (97 km) per hour but, in a dive, can reach a speed of 175 miles (282 km) per hour.

5 The green heron uses bait to fish. It drops an insect on the surface of the water and grabs any fish that approaches the bait.

6 European house sparrows are the most common wild birds. Domestic chickens are even more common and outnumber humans.

Glossary

canopy (KA-nuh-pee) The branches and leaves on the very top layer of a tree.

coverts (KOH-vertz) The rows of feathers that overlap the flight feathers on a bird's wings and tail.

drag (DRAG) The push of a stream of air against a flying bird.

endangered (in-DAYN-jerd) Describes an animal species whose numbers are so small that it is in danger of becoming extinct.

forage (FOR-ij) To search for food.

fused (FYOOZD) Joined very tightly as if melted together.

glide (GLYD) To fly using air streams and without wings beating.

hover (HUH-ver) To remain in the same place by fluttering wings.

keratin (KER-uh-tun) A horny substance or protein found in dinosaur scales, bird feathers, and human hair.

molt (MOHLT) To shed old, worn feathers so that new, healthy feathers can grow in their place.

nocturnal (nok-TUR-nul) Describes animals that are active at night and sleep during the day.

ornithologist (or-nih-THAH-luh-jist) A scientist who studies birds.

plume (PLOOM) A large, showy feather.

predator (PREH-duh-ter) An animal that kills and eats other animals.

prey (PRAY) An animal that is killed and eaten by another animal.

remiges (RI-muh-jiz) The large contour feathers on a bird's wings that support the bird in flight.

rectrices (REK-tre-ses) The large tail feathers that help to control and stabilize a flying bird.

roosting (ROOST-ing) Perching, usually on a branch, to rest or sleep.

scavenger (SKA-ven-jur) An animal that eats dead animals or animal waste.

shaft (SHAFT) The hollow, central stem of a feather.

soaring (SAWR-ing) Flying high and upward, using air currents and almost no wing movement.

sternum (STIR-num) The large central section of the breastbone.

terrestrial (tuh-RES-tree-ul) Describes animals, including birds, that live on land.

vortex (VOR-teks) A spinning flow of air that sucks anything nearby toward its center.

wetlands (WET-landz) A low area of land that is soaked with water or covered in shallow water.

wingspan (WING-span) The measurement or distance from the tip of one wing to the tip of the other.

Index

Websites

Due to the changing nature of Internet links, PowerKids Press has developed an online list of websites related to the subject of this book. This site is updated regularly. Please use this link to access the list:
www.powerkidslinks.com/disc/fly/